Dog Days

Dog Days

Linda Coggin

zero books

Winchester, UK
Washington, USA

First published by Zero Books, 2011
Zero Books is an imprint of John Hunt Publishing Ltd., Laurel House, Station Approach, Alresford, Hants, SO24 9JH, UK
office1@o-books.net
www.o-books.com

For distributor details and how to order please visit the 'Ordering' section on our website.

ISBN: 978 1 84694 547 2

A CIP catalogue record for this book is available from the British Library.

Design: Lee Nash

Printed in the UK by CPI Antony Rowe
Printed in the USA by Offset Paperback Mfrs, Inc

We operate a distinctive and ethical publishing philosophy in all areas of our business, from our global network of authors to production and worldwide distribution.

CONTENTS

Acknowledgments

I would like to thank Johnny Bull for his loyal encouragement and advice and for his beautiful illustrations. Tariq and Emma for seeing something I had not and without whom this book would never be. John Hunt for publishing it. John Freeman for his help and guidance. Susie Alexander, Elinor Bagenal, Roland Challis, Matt Cutts and Mike Redpath, my fellow Random Poets, for their friendship, support and inspiration. And finally, Mark Fisher for his diligent copy-editing.

For Chloë and Phoebe

Dog Day Afternoon

On dog day afternoons I grow a tail
and become a cur of undetermined heritage
tugging at codgers' trouser cuffs
roughing it with tattered papers
from wretch to top bitch
an über pooch heralding death
with a bark, who knows how

to park a car, wash a floor
iron a shirt
flirt with the man next door
mix a cocktail or two – but obviously
wouldn't let on
to the other dogs.

A morphological transformation, a sensation
part mutt part alsatian doing the dog dance
and sitting for no one in particular
burying a bone, chasing the cat up
a tree – peeing against a lamp post
fetching a stick at considerable speed
disappearing into a landscape of flowers
and not hearing their cries when they call me home.

Fluff in the Ideal Home

There's fluff in the bedroom
the yoghurt pots have beards
weird antibiotics live
in the clothes which mutate on the floor
a knicker mountain has formed
a doll slag heap
and fluff replicates
at an alarming rate.

Displaced socks seek out
the Mothercare pyjamas which
drift around in the dust
whilst somewhere
five miles down
in the carpet's crust
undetected organisms eke out
a slow existence.

Inferior felt tips mix
with the nano bacteria
in the sediment of the bed
and groups of immigrant shoes kick
alongside something
which looks dead.
very small crocodiles make out
in the crawl space –

Where does all that fluff
come from for heaven's sake?
They say it's flakes of skin.

Take care – someone might
collect it all
and make little models
of you.

My Dad – Midas

I can hear Dad down in the halls
bellowing grief for all he loved –
all that his roving hands had touched
and I, the favourite once, am banished
to my room, forgotten, as my sisters
lie on their burnished beds.

The light takes on an orange tinge.
Two maids are caught turning sheets,
arms bent in duty, faces gleaming,
their fingers printed in the dust.
I want him to see me but he does not come.

I apply leaf so paper thin it falls like
feathers on my skin. Gold powder flies
into the air, rests upon my hair, my cheeks –
breasts brim with amber milk.
Now my knees – smudged here but they
will have to do.
My legs, the turn of my heel,
the curl of my toes, gilded and rooted
to the ground.

And when I'm found
they'll think he loved me too.

I hold my breath

I'm Daddy's Little Golden Girl.

Job Exchange

The waitress, who was really
an actress
wondered, as she stirred the cup of cappuccino.
if Al Capone had ever been played
by Al Pacino.

The janitor, who was really
a poet
pushed a perambulator in iambic pentameter
for the lonely old lady when
she lost her key.

The judge, who was really
a mother
sent prisoners guilty of felony
to bed for ten years
without any tea.

The gardener, who was really
a musician
planted adagios with the radicchios
in the Titanic
Memorial dome.

The sous-chef, who was really
a magician
became a sorcerer in the kitchen
with balsamic vinegar
and brimstone.

And the husband, who was really

an adulterer
wrote missives in pheromone from Congress
to his lover who was really
a waitress.

Dead Man Walking

Given by women in widow's weeds
and mourning daughters in cashmere
you wear them all –
the singlets, slippers, soft hats
windbreakers, jackets and the endless
pile of socks that once adorned
their husbands and fathers.
Do you feel the bedside manner
of the doctor as you button up his shirt
inside your cardboard box?
Can you sense the girl who sat
on the knees of those slacks?
Does the stockbroker's jersey
give you confidence as you go
on your noctambulist's odyssey?
And do any of these women recognise
Someone in you as you walk
past them in the street?
Of course not – they would divert their eyes –
afraid that you would
ask for money.

Letting Go

We let her go
like a large fish
grasping for air
all fight gone.
We made small gestures
of comfort
water on the lips
morphine in the veins
pillows banked.
We combed her hair.
And when we weren't looking
she slipped away
back into the dark waters
of the night.

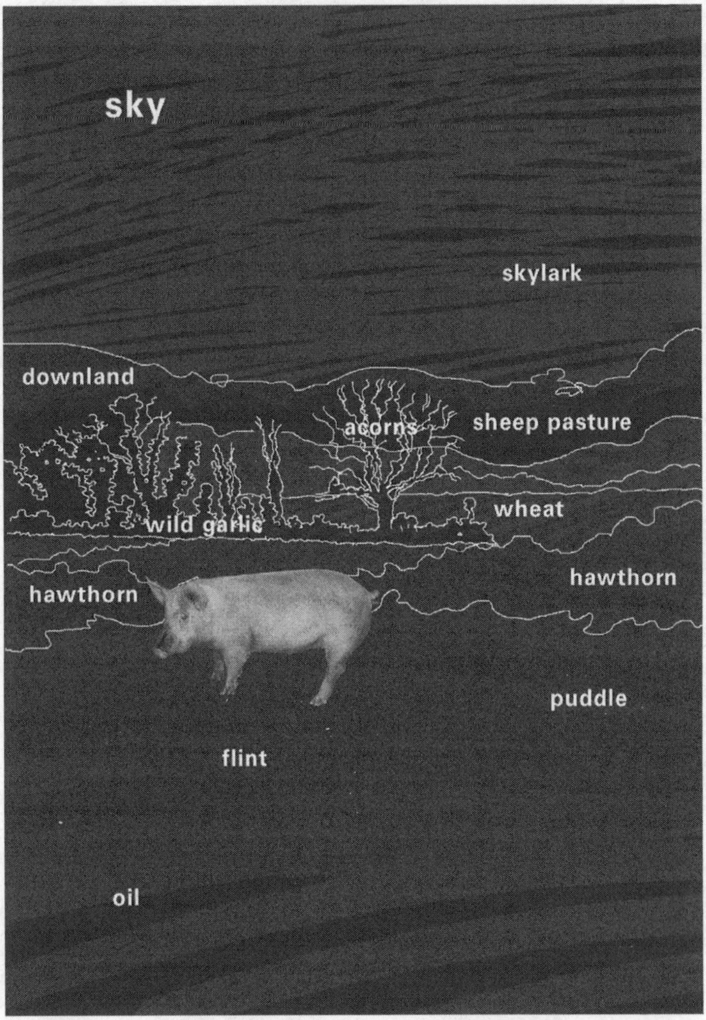
sky
skylark
downland
acorns
sheep pasture
wheat
wild garlic
hawthorn
hawthorn
puddle
flint
oil

Fork Lift

Within the tin shed
little pink chops are fed
and prize pork pies
bred for their improved size
carry with pride
the label of Animal Welfare
on their side.
Able to eat, as they please,
free from hunger
and free from disease
no fear of Armageddon for gammon
or green back bacon
no feeling of panic
in these ordered, organic lives
just pig like Stepford wives
just food
within the tin shed
no host or hostess
no stress, no Prozac in the strawsack
only double oats and men
in off white coats
as Freedom Food meets Sigmund Freud.

And when they leave to meet the knife
serenaded by hired hands
playing Strauss on the mandolin
only one pig sees
the colours of summer
the ever stretching green fields
and blue skies, hears the fine

song of the sky lark
composed for a beautiful day
and wonders about her life
these pearls before swine.
Then she joins the line
with her communard in lard
and the trucks roll away.

Entirely Spider

It broods in the folds
of the nightdress –
huge, as if it wears an overcoat
– as dark as dreams.
I shudder and sleep in the other room
there is nothing sadder than
being single and having
to deal with a large bug.

Later, when life becomes
too short to dust
and I have found other fears
I keep good company with one.
Through the borrowed view
of the bedpost
I watch her dance attendance
repair and tidy her beautiful web
nibbling at her trussed hors d'oeuvre
saving herself for the Big One
her Mr. Right whom she devours
after a night of spinning passion
her just dessert.

Curled like a cat
she fills the corner
her egg sac casting a vast shadow
across the ceiling
she ceases to scurry
instead she watches and waits
her web slack with time

and misuse.
Now, as winter approaches she is ready
for her long descent.
She clings to her clever thread
my daughters screaming as she wearily
passes them
I cajole and re-assure
I place her in the palm to prove a point
and now, close up
she seems much smaller than I thought.

Shelf Life

We clustered snugly together
like clutches of warm buns
in an oven
and once a month
when proven
one of us would leave
in anticipation of meeting
the finishing touches.
I remember the one
who would become my brother
not properly formed,
missing a chromosome
don't go
we warned
stay with us
but he went
without fuss, still viable
and able with pills
to live in a home.
My sister
an exquisite complexity
of cells
that would foretell
her large feet and surly moods
left early
and then the others,
expectant, with our mother's
tears and her mother's smile
met no one on the way.
We who were left
diminished through the years

till I
the last to leave
finished off the chores
made sure the room was clean
had the foresight
to turn off the light
and close the oven doors.

Lilith

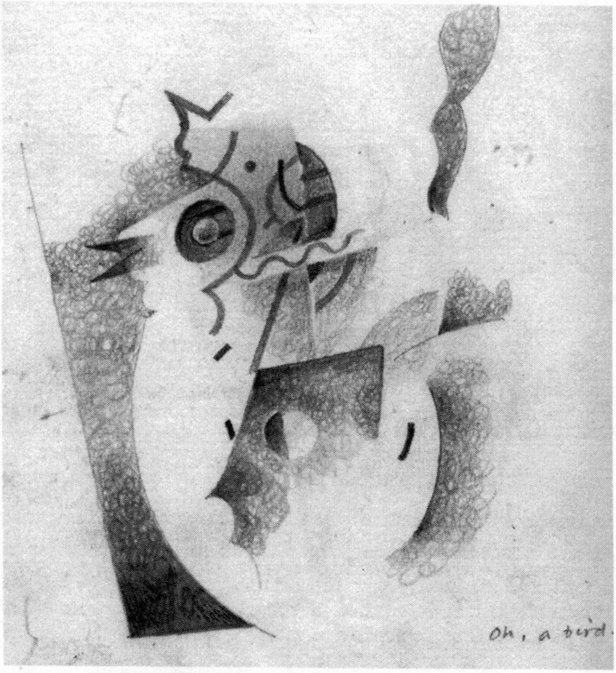

The new feathers fitted
uncomfortably around her body
suppressing the natural curves
of her breasts, thighs and buttocks.
Instead of her juicy lips which before
had planted sighs and kisses
on delighted cheeks
she had – a beak.
Her feet, which had danced
to the beat of time
were constricted into
sharp, tight claws

but her eyes –
dark, bright, shining
and reliant
still saw –
everything.
She watched soft, compliant Eve
smoothing Adam's bed
she eyed the apple
tempting for that pie
that Eve was so good at making.
She decided not to stick around
to see what happened to those boys
she had men to visit
in their dreams.

Dress Making

Her mother pins the hated
seersucker frock, as she, elevated
on a table turns
like the ballerina
on top of a jewel box.
The hem hangs crooked,
mulish, around her knees.
Knocking the pins to the floor,
the mother cries.
The girl stands, her lips tacked shut.
Later other vignettes
get pinned to her chest
like interfacing hidden
in the collar of a best dress.

Now she wonders what moments
her children will wear?
Will it be the vase
hurled at the closing door,
the tears in the car-park
at the broken jar of marmalade?
Arrested moments
tailor made, not easily discarded
but worn as a coat
buttoned, revered – double breasted.

The Father's Race

The school bell tolls as they jockey
at the line, casual, acting the goat
wishing they were dead or down the pub
still time to do that deal –
but then they're off and scorching grass
as fast as squibs across the turf
past sons and daughters who perch
in mirth and dig each other in the ribs.

Brogues and trainers blaze the furlong
outrunning hares, with lungs protesting.
Men in nightmares running nude
with limbs of lead and feet in glue.
A cry goes up – a man is down.
Embarrassed as his father falls
one boy goes red and turns away.

As the first men pass the line to yells
and shouts, it seems that flowers sprout
within the empty grass that separates
the winners from the rest
and insects brave the crossing
of the track and big black birds sail and tack.

Then short of breath with barrel chests
the others totter in behind.
These are the slack, the flimsy men
the unstrung heroes of the field
the real winners of the race who
brave the torment of the chase

to whom the anthem should be sung.
For these are sons of fathers
who had never run for them.

Not as a Friend

I really wanted to be your friend
I wanted to be there – your age
in those old photos you showed me
to be part of your group by the beach huts
with the lads you said all died
later in the war.
To be in that dinghy with the pirate flag
sailing down the creek, my uncle as a small boy.
Eating cornets on the sand. Playing cricket
by the dew pond.
Whatever age you were it was before
I came into the world
but I can recognise in the pictures
the shape of my mouth
the way you stand awkwardly
on one leg like I do.
So in a way I had been there
only not as a friend as such.

Alice Dunn - an obituary

Alice Dunn was one of eleven
born at number four.
Three times a day she walked
to the school and as a rule
three times on the Sabbath
to the Parish church where
she was christened then married
later buried her
children and which she would clean
for forty two years.
She went into service at the age
of fifteen, for sixty years
at the house on the green of
the village where she was born
and for a peppercorn rent
still lived next door
in the cottage at number four.

Alice Dunn enjoyed playing whist.

A few years back she moved
to number six, next to the school.
It must have been the gypsy in her soul.

Wedding shoes

The day I marry, my bridesmaid
curled inside my womb
my home made dress divorcing
at the seam, next to the groom
I chose because
I liked his shoes,
I think of the pros in the dockside bars
who sat in rows their legs
crossed neatly at the thigh
their fare inscribed upon their soles.

My bridesmaid kicks.
We've not yet met. Later she will
tell me the earth's weight but now
she causes a hook to fly undone,
a vent to form, an expanse of girth
to be revealed.

He'd worn black, with leather uppers
only now they're patent
so bright I see my knickers in the toes.
He wears some re-incarnation of a once
more modest flower in his lapel
and as I hitch my skirts and kneel
I feel that all the congregation see
stuck to the bottom of my pretty mules
the label – Dolcis, fourteen ninety nine.

School trip to The Museum

(homage to George Mac Kay)

They went to the Museum with toffee filled pockets.
Norman found a manatee and listened to a whale
on the telephone.
Keith waited by the mini-beasts for Simon
who didn't show.

Lucy watched a film on life in the womb all morning
and later
had trouble with her small intestine.

No one took notes.

George played three rounds on the heart beat machine
he died twice.
Where did they find Samuel?
They found him with the nine-banded armadillo
all small and wet eyed.

They ate Angel cake and bought bug-eyes from the shop
Samuel's broke on the journey home.

The Invasion of the Memorial Seat

The benches look outwards towards
the city – so many of them
that movement is restricted
an open air waiting room
where we too can rest in peace
eat a sandwich, and contemplate
our own demise.

Some seats have formed splinter groups
Blocking former foot paths,
edging around playing fields
mingling with the trolleys by
the supermarkets – Remembering Mum
A spot she loved so much.

Unthreatened by memorial saplings
they appear at roadsides, on dangerous bends
even up trees themselves,
a perfect place for us to survey
the horizon and mourn
the ancient woodland destroyed
supplying wood for all those benches.

Air Borne

Jack Tar, mariner, bosun, coxswain
able seaman, lighterman, ferryman
and captain
sea dogs once now
sea lords flying
cruising and coasting
mewing and crying
plying for fish
they tease and bait
sea farer
now voyager
they circumnavigate.

So how many ways does a sailor die?
Torpedoed, capsized
washed ashore
trawling, brawling
with mates for a whore
in Shanghai.
Cold in Archangel
and out of reach
or covered in flies
on a bone-china beach.

Then what becomes of
the sailor's souls,
these birds and gulls,
at their demise?
Tarred and feathered
weathered and dumb.

Strangled in plastic
Is what they become.

Memory Moth

As a moth I have become your mind
making small holes in your memory
that you cannot darn, so that when
you are remembering, you fall into them
and confused, clutch at the sides
hoping to pull yourself clear.

I am your memory moth
fluttering down the years
flying from memories before you
can form the words to describe them.

Whilst the light is still turned on
I can agitate you, confuse you by
changing direction when I fly.
If you were to turn off the light
I would be still.

One day soon, you and I will
Have our wings burnt
And dissolve into a cloud of dust.

Closing Down

Closing down
everything must go
a lifetime of pastimes
going for a song.
A last minute decision
hoes, rakes and dibbers
that have no use
and do not belong
and tools of precision
that shaky hands
can no longer prescribe.

Tins of bits
and jars for pieces,
now confused,
and packets of seeds
stored for a generation
and not used
too many to mention
and describe.

Carefully labelled boxes
and parts of railway tracks
charts and manuals
annuals, maps and almanacs.
Offer ends soon
owner out of town
everything must go
my father is
closing down.

Contemporary culture has eliminated both the concept of the public and the figure of the intellectual. Former public spaces – both physical and cultural – are now either derelict or colonized by advertising. A cretinous anti-intellectualism presides, cheerled by expensively educated hacks in the pay of multinational corporations who reassure their bored readers that there is no need to rouse themselves from their interpassive stupor. The informal censorship internalized and propagated by the cultural workers of late capitalism generates a banal conformity that the propaganda chiefs of Stalinism could only ever have dreamt of imposing. Zer0 Books knows that another kind of discourse – intellectual without being academic, popular without being populist – is not only possible: it is already flourishing, in the regions beyond the striplit malls of so-called mass media and the neurotically bureaucratic halls of the academy. Zer0 is committed to the idea of publishing as a making public of the intellectual. It is convinced that in the unthinking, blandly consensual culture in which we live, critical and engaged theoretical reflection is more important than ever before.